MARK

The Beginning of the Gospel

Peter Bolt and
Tony Payne

FAITHWALK
BIBLE STUDIES

CROSSWAY BOOKS • WHEATON, ILLINOIS
A DIVISION OF GOOD NEWS PUBLISHERS

15	14	13	12	11	10	09	08	07	06	05	04	03	02	01	00
15	14	13	12	11	10	9	8	7	6	5	4	3	2	1	

Contents

How to Make the Most
of These Studies

1. What Is an Interactive Bible Study?

These "interactive" Bible studies are a bit like a guided tour of a famous city. The studies will take you through the Gospel of Mark, pointing out things along the way, filling in background details, and suggesting avenues for further exploration. But there is also time for you to do some sightseeing of your own—to wander off, have a good look for yourself, and form your own conclusions.

In other words, we have designed these studies to fall halfway between a sermon and a set of unadorned Bible study questions. We want to provide stimulation and input and point you in the right direction, while leaving you to do a lot of the exploration and discovery yourself.

We hope that these studies will stimulate a lot of interaction—interaction with the Bible, with the teaching material, with your own ideas, with other people in discussion, and with God as you talk to Him about it all.

2. The Format

Each study contains sections of text to introduce, summarize, suggest, and provoke. Interspersed throughout the teaching are three types of "interaction," each with its own symbol:

STARTING OUT

Questions to help you think about society and your own experience in a way that tunes you in to the issues being raised by the Bible passage.

FINDING TRUTH

Questions to help you investigate key parts of the Bible.

GOING FURTHER

Questions to help you think through the implications of your discoveries.

When you come to one of these symbols, you'll know that it's time to do some work on your own.

3. Suggestions for Individual Study

▲ Before you begin, pray that God will open your eyes to what He is saying in Mark's Gospel and give you the strength to do something about it. You may be spurred to pray again at the end of the study.

▲ Work through the study, following the directions as you go. Write in the spaces provided.

▲ Resist the temptation to skip over the *Starting Out, Finding Truth,* and *Going Further* sections. It is important to think about the sections of text (rather than just accepting them as true) and to ponder the implications for your life. Writing these things down is a valuable way to get your thoughts working.

▲ Take what opportunities you can to talk with others about what you've learned.

4. Suggestions for Group Study

▲ Much of what we have suggested above applies to group study as well. The studies are suitable for structured Bible study or cell groups, as well as for more informal pairs and threesomes.

Get together with one or more friends and work on the studies at your own pace. You don't need the formal structure of a "group" to gain maximum benefit.

▲ It is vital that group members work through the study themselves *before* the group meets. The group discussion can take place comfortably in an hour (depending on how sidetracked you get!), but only if all the members have done the work and are familiar with the material.

▲ Spend most of the group time discussing the "interactive" sections—*Starting Out, Finding Truth,* and *Going Further.* Reading all the text together would take too long and should be unnecessary if group members have done their preparation. You may wish to underline and read aloud particular paragraphs or sections of text that you think are important.

▲ The role of the group leader is to direct the course of the discussion and try to draw the threads together at the end. This will mean a little extra preparation—underlining important sections of text to emphasize, deciding which questions are worth concentrating on, being sure of the main thrust of the study. Leaders will also probably want to decide approximately how long they'd like to spend on each part.

▲ We haven't included an "answer guide" to the questions in the studies. This is a deliberate move—we want to give you a guided tour of Mark, not a lecture. There is more than enough in the text we have written and the questions we have asked to point you in what we think is the right direction. The rest is up to you.

▲ For more input, see "Tips for Leaders" at the end of the book.

5. Before You Begin

We recommend that before you start on study 1, you take the time to read right through Mark in one sitting. This will give you a feel for the direction and purpose of the whole book and will help you greatly in looking at each passage in its context.

"At That Time, Jesus"

MARK 1:1-15

Was Jesus a great prophet and teacher? Was He merely one in a long line of inspired individuals, including Buddha and Mohammed? Did He travel to England as a child? Is He more popular than the Beatles?

These days, it seems possible to find as many different "Jesuses" as brands of soft drink. Every year there's another book about the "authentic" Jesus. All the authors have their own theory, and they all present it as the most obvious and plausible one. Most have this in common: They disagree with traditional Christianity. How do we deal with this huge range of opinions?

Jesus was a historical figure who lived and died in the first century. He was also a powerful teacher who, in the centuries following His lifetime, has influenced the lives of millions of people from many different nationalities and personal backgrounds. No serious-minded person would disagree with these statements. Yet the full meaning and significance of Jesus remains a contentious issue. Who was He really? And what was He all about?

 STARTING OUT

What do people say about Jesus? What opinions do you hear in the media, at work, or from family and friends? On what do people base their opinions? Jot down a few answers.

If we want to know the truth about the earthly life of Jesus, there is only one place to turn. We must read and study the Gospels, for they are the only reliable source of detailed information about Him.

The Gospel of Mark is probably the earliest of the four Gospels, and was written while many of those involved in the events (as participants or eyewitnesses) were still alive. It is a remarkable book, and not only because of its subject matter. The more we read Mark's account of Jesus, the more we are entranced by what a great story it is and by how well it is told.

Many of us are not used to reading Mark or any of the other Gospels as one continuous story. Instead, we tend to regard the Gospels as collections of lots of different stories that don't have much to do with each other. We're familiar with stories about healings and exorcisms, about John the Baptist, about miracles and parables, about arguments with Jewish leaders, and of course about Jesus' death and resurrection. Yet many of us have grown up with these Gospel stories without pausing to think that there might be a connection between all these different incidents, that the Gospel author might be trying to tell a big story of which all the different episodes are only part.

We can be like people who know a movie only by the advertisements they see on TV. We have a rough idea of what the Gospel is about and have seen the highlights, but we haven't yet grasped how the whole thing holds together and what the overall point is. In fact, we aren't even sure which "movie" the episodes come from, since there are four versions of Christ's life, each written from a slightly different perspective and each containing particular emphases.

These studies are like a trip to see one of these "movies"—the Gospel of Mark. We're not going to simply look at a grab bag of highlights; we're going to see how the whole story fits together, how the characters relate to each other, how one episode flows into the next, and how Mark presents us with a unique portrait of Jesus.

As we do so, we'll see that the Jesus of Mark's Gospel is not only surprising and intriguing—He also fulfills all our grandest dreams.

Let us begin where all stories begin: at the beginning.

The Beginning of the Gospel

According to its opening words, Mark's book will tell its readers about "the beginning of the gospel of Jesus Christ, the Son of God." Mark is written for those living after the time of Jesus, to tell them how the Christian message originated. Where did it come from, this "Good News" about a crucified Messiah? What were the events that started it all? Who was this Jesus? What was He all about? And what was He supposed to have done?

Mark immediately identifies Jesus as "the Christ" and "the Son of God." We are so used to these words that we barely pause to consider what they mean. However, for Mark's original readers, these were words full of significance.

Christ, for example, is not Jesus' surname. The word *Christ* is the Greek equivalent of the Hebrew word *messiah,* which means "anointed one" and described the kings of Israel. Over time it came to signify the long-awaited King God had promised, who would one day come to defeat all of Israel's enemies and bring in a new age of prosperity and peace.

"Son of God" basically means the same thing. It was another way of describing the kings of Israel (2 Sam. 7:14; Ps. 2:7; 89:26-27) and so is another way of referring to the Christ or Messiah. It is a somewhat confusing title for Christians because we are used to calling Jesus "God the Son"—that is, the second person of the Trinity. But these are two slightly different things. God the Son has always been at the Father's side, from all eternity. When Jesus was born as a man and lived and died and rose from the dead, He became the "Son of God" in this additional sense as well—that is, He became the long-awaited Messiah or Christ of Israel.

From the outset, then, Mark tells his readers something that the characters in the story (e.g., the disciples) will take some time to discover. We know from the start that Jesus—the central character—is the Christ (or Messiah), the Son of God. From the start, we know that this is no ordinary story but concerns the King of all the earth!

What Happens Next

The royal coach, pulled by four immaculate horses, draws up to the entrance of the great hall. The red carpet is out. Dignitaries wait nervously in the hope of recognition or even a handshake. The crowd strains forward to catch a glimpse. The footman opens the door . . . and out steps . . .

We all know what happens next. We all know whom to expect. The signs and trappings of royalty are unmistakable.

Yet when Jesus began His public ministry, what did people expect? What were the signs? Was the red carpet out?

Jesus the Messiah certainly did not arrive in a vacuum, unexpected and unannounced. On the contrary, He had been expected for hundreds of years. And if we are to understand anything about Jesus, we must understand something of the expectations that surrounded His arrival and the kingdom He would bring.

In fact, Mark begins his story by telling us from the Old Testament just who was expected and what was meant to happen once He arrived.

What Happens Next . . . According to the Old Testament

 FINDING TRUTH

Read Malachi 3:1-5. (Mark 1:2 is a quote from Malachi 3:1.)
1. What does Malachi prophesy will happen first?

A messanger to prepare the way

2. What is supposed to happen after that?

He will come to judge and purify (especially the priests).

Read Isaiah 40:1-11. (Mark 1:3 is a quote from Isaiah 40:3.)
3. What does Isaiah prophesy will happen first?

A voice will cry out in the wilderness to prepare the way for the Lord.

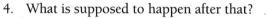

4. What is supposed to happen after that?

The glory of the Lord will be revealed.

5. How would you summarize the promise of these Old Testament verses?

What Happens Next . . . According to John

As soon as Mark finishes quoting these prophecies, he introduces John the Baptist (Mark 1:4-8).

 FINDING TRUTH

Read Mark 1:4-8.

1. Why did the people come to John? What were they looking for?

To be baptized and have their sins forgiven.

2. John is portrayed by Mark as the "messenger" of the Old Testament prophecies. According to John's message, what will happen next?

A greater "man" will come and he will baptize with the Holy Spirit.

3. According to the Old Testament prophecies we looked at above, who was supposed to come after John?

The Lord

"Baptism with the Spirit"

Baptism "with the Holy Spirit" (1:8) refers neither to Christian baptismal practices nor to what Pentecostals refer to as the "second blessing." Both of these interpretations try to read later church phenomena back into the Gospel. Instead, we must understand this reference to baptism in light of the situation in Jesus' time. Notice that John compares a symbol ("I baptize you with water") with the reality ("He will baptize you with the Holy Spirit"). "Baptism" simply means a washing, and is a natural symbol for cleansing or purification. "Baptism with the Holy Spirit" is the cleansing or purifying that God will do. This is what people wanted (1:4-5) and what the Old Testament had promised.

What Happens Next . . . According to God

The words are barely out of John's mouth when Mark introduces the very One John had been speaking about:

> *At that time Jesus came from Nazareth in Galilee and was baptized by John in the Jordan.*
>
> —Mark 1:9

In a dramatic scene, Jesus is endowed with the Holy Spirit and hears a voice from heaven, saying, "You are my Son, whom I love; with you I am well pleased."

This short sentence seems a straightforward thing to say. God is declaring from heaven that He loves His Son, and that He is very pleased with Him. But there is more to it than that. God is repeating words that He had spoken many hundreds of years earlier in the Old Testament. God is quoting from two Old Testament passages, one about His Son whom He loves, and another about a "Servant" who would receive the Spirit and be well-pleasing to God.

 FINDING TRUTH

Read Psalm 2.

1. What should happen once God's Son, the King of Israel, is established on His throne?

The whole earth becomes Jesus'
The people should serve the Lord with fear

Read Isaiah 42:1-4.

2. When the Spirit-filled Servant arrives, what will happen next?

He will bring justice to every nation

3. There are three other passages about this Servant in Isaiah. Quickly read them. What do they tell us about the ministry of the Servant?

▲ Isaiah 49:1-7

People will praise God because of Jesus. He will be a light to save people

▲ Isaiah 50:4-11

He will strengthen the weary

▲ Isaiah 52:13–53:12

He will succeed and be honoured He gave his life willingly for the forgiveness of sins.

What Happens Next . . . According to Jesus

In this climate of expectation, with all these promises and prophecies in the air, and with John the Baptist pointing to Him as the One they'd been waiting for, Jesus begins to proclaim His message: "The time has come. . . . The kingdom of God is near. Repent and believe the good news!" (Mark 1:14-15).

According to Jesus, the time has finally come. The prophecies are about to be fulfilled. The long-awaited kingdom is near. And since this is all about to happen, it is a time for urgent and immediate action.

According to Jesus, two things will happen next: 1) the kingdom will come; and 2) His hearers will have to make up their minds as to how to respond—either accepting His message (by repenting and believing) or rejecting it.

 **GOING FURTHER**

1. If someone asked you, "Who is Jesus?" how would you reply? How has this study affected your answer?

2. Imagine that you have never read Mark's Gospel nor even heard the story of Jesus. What do you expect to happen next as Mark's Gospel unfolds?

3. Why should every person alive take a good look at Jesus?

"As One Who Had Authority"

MARK 1:16–3:35

So far in Mark's Gospel, we have been awaiting the arrival of the King. Mark has told us from the outset that his book is all about Jesus, the King, the Messiah. We have been reminded of the Old Testament expectations and have heard the testimony of John the Baptist and even of God Himself at Jesus' baptism.

Now the King has stepped from the carriage onto the waiting red carpet and announced His arrival ("the kingdom of God is near"). One thing remains: What will the King do? How will He act? How will He wield His royal power?

In this next section of Mark's Gospel, we not only begin to see the royal authority of Jesus the Messiah in action, we also see Him start to interact with His subjects. Mark introduces us to the different characters who will figure in the dramatic story to follow.

Four Encounters with Authority

 FINDING TRUTH

(If you are studying in a group, you may want to break into four smaller groups and take one of the following passages each, then report back.)

1. The fishermen

Read Mark 1:16-20.

a. What does Jesus promise to do for these men?

He will teach us to "catch" men.
"bring in"

b. If they follow Him, what will be the consequences?

They must leave everything familiar behind - family, jobs

c. What does this encounter tell us about Jesus the King?

Commanding presence - none question him.
He gives a choice.
We must obey "now" - they did not do anything hasty

2. The synagogue

Read Mark 1:21-28.

a. Why are people impressed by Jesus in Capernaum?

He taught with authority
Taught at the level of the common people.

b. What does the evil spirit know that the crowd does not know?

That Jesus was god's messenger

c. What does this encounter tell us about Jesus the King?

He has the authority over evil.
Favoured by God

3. The sick

Read Mark 1:29-39.

a. How is Jesus' authority shown in this section?

By his healing touch and command over the demons.
Followed god's plan and not people's demand.

b. From Jesus' actions and words, what did He think His mission was all about?

To teach and reach as many people as possible.
To cure and to heal — spiritually also.

4. *The leper*

Read Mark 1:40-45.

a. Why do you think the leper was hesitant about asking for healing?

He was an outcast and perhaps Jesus would treat him the same.

b. What do you find surprising about this incident?

Jesus said do not tell and yet the man did.
Jesus knew how little acceptance of him there was — the priest had to confirm the healing.

c. What does Jesus' encounter with the leper tell us about the sort of king He is?

Not proud — told him not to talk.
Caring — took pity.
Told leper to give thanks to God via sacrifice.

These passages certainly show what a remarkable person Jesus was. The fishermen left their ordinary life, their work, and their families, and at this stage they did not even know where Jesus was heading! There must have been something compelling about Jesus to command such a response. Obviously His healings drew people's attention—but notice that although Jesus was able to heal and had sympathy for the ill, healing was not His primary interest. He left the huge crowd to go farther afield with His preaching about the coming kingdom (vv. 38-39).

In many respects, we modern readers are distracted by the fact that Jesus could heal at all. We are so struck by His power that we can easily overlook how astounding it was for Him to *touch* someone with leprosy, someone defiled and "unclean" under the religious law of the time. The leper certainly did not expect a touch from Jesus; he doubted Jesus' *willingness* to heal (v. 40), not His ability to do so.

Jesus has already been contrasted with the religious leaders of the day (v. 22). In the next series of stories, this contrast becomes open conflict.

Authority Opposed

 FINDING TRUTH

Read Mark 2:1-12.

1. What is the source of Jesus' authority?

    God

2. What is Jesus' authority for?

    To forgive sins

3. What were the responses to Jesus' words (and the actions that backed them up)?

    They were amazed — they praised God
    Pharisees felt Jesus was blaspheming

The "Son of Man" is how Jesus refers to Himself. It could be that this is just a roundabout way of speaking, much as one can use "one" in referring to oneself. It is hardly a coincidence, however, that the "Son of Man" was also the name given to a man in Daniel 7 who came to God (Dan. 7:13) and was given the kingdom of God (Dan. 7:14; compare Dan. 2:44), thereby gaining authority over all people.

4. Read the following passages in Mark and fill in the table

	What opposition does Jesus face?	(If relevant) How does Jesus answer the opposition?
2:13-17	Eating with outcasts.	Well people do not need a doctor.
2:18-20	His disciples do not fast.	They will once the "bride groom" has left the wedding
2:23-28	Disciples picked corn on the Sabbath	Sabbath for the good of man — He is Lord of Sabbath
3:1-6	Healing on the Sabbath — paralysed hand.	What is the law re Sabbath Heal or harm, save or destroy life.
3:20-21, 31-34	His family try to take charge	All who obey God are His family

Overall — laws should not be kept too rigidly for their own sake.

To sum up: What is the difference between Jesus' attitude and that of His opponents?

Jesus cares for people, the opponents "care" about the laws
Humble vs self-righteous

Read Mark 3:22-29.
In this scene, the religious leaders oppose Jesus to His face. They question the source of His authority (vv. 22, 30).

5. How does Jesus' riddle answer their charge (vv. 23-27)?

It would be pointless for Satan to destroy himself

6. Why does Jesus give them such a stern warning (vv. 28-30)?

The people were saying that His Spirit — the Holy Spirit was evil.

Blaspheming the Holy Spirit

This passage has often worried Christians. "What if I blaspheme the Holy Spirit?"

We need to look carefully at what is actually being said. Jesus was accused of being from Satan. This is utter blasphemy, for Jesus' authority does not come from Satan but from God. Jesus, the Son, the Servant of the Lord, is the one upon whom the Spirit came (1:9-11). If people reject Him, they "blaspheme the Spirit." Jesus is the Son of Man, with the authority to forgive sins on earth (2:10). If the religious leaders reject Him, they reject the only source of forgiveness and will therefore remain guilty of eternal sin.

Reacting to Authority

The people of Jesus' day were confronted with a choice. They had traditionally found out about God by following their authorized religious leaders. But now a new teacher had arrived on the scene, one who oozed authority in everything He said and did. How would they react? Would their amazement lead them to "repent and believe the good news," as Jesus had challenged them to do?

These are the questions waiting to be answered as we read on.

 GOING FURTHER

1. From what we have read so far in Mark, what was Jesus offering people if they followed Him?

    Forgiveness and eternal life.

2. What does Jesus offer us today that religious leaders cannot equal?

Forgiveness, peace, eternal life, the "Way" to God's kingdom.

3. What is radical about Jesus' authority?

It is not granted by man and is therefore absolute — it is from God.
Speaks with God's power.

4. What is the stern warning that arises from the passages we have studied?

The only means of salvation is Jesus Christ. We reject him at our peril.

Obey God's word — prepare for Jesus' return.

Be careful of misjudging and being self-righteous.
Obey the Holy Spirit

"This Is What the Kingdom Will Be Like"

MARK 4:1-34

 STARTING OUT

1. Through the media and your daily contact with people, what kinds of things do people hope that the future will hold for them?

2. What do they hope the future will hold for their children?

3. What do you think are the chances that their hopes will be realized?

4. What is your own most pressing hope for the future? What do you long for and dream about most?

Most human dreams remain just that—dreams. In fact, the harder we work toward fulfilling our dreams, the more elusive they can be.

Jesus also had a dream for the future, except it was not so much a dream as a plan. He knew it would happen, and the challenge He put before people was to believe that it was going to happen and to change their lives accordingly.

What was Jesus expecting? What sort of future was He banking on? And how did He expect it to come about?

Chapter 4 of Mark's Gospel has Jesus beginning to explain what the future kingdom of God will be like, and why only some will enter it.

The Prophecies of the Kingdom

Once again, to understand this next section of Mark we need to acquaint ourselves with the Old Testament background that lies behind it. The prophets of the Old Testament had great hopes for the future kingdom God would establish. Let us explore some of those hopes.

 FINDING TRUTH

1. Read the following passages. What does each passage expect will happen?

   ▲ Daniel 2:44

   ▲ Daniel 7:13-14

   ▲ Daniel 7:17-18, 26-27

   ▲ Daniel 12:1-4

2. How will this kingdom meet the longings of humanity?

3. Read the following verses. When was the kingdom of God expected?

   ▲ Daniel 12:1-4, 8-9, 13

   ▲ Mark 1:14-15

Many Old Testament passages describe the kingdom to come, and we have looked at only a sample. The people of Israel knew that God did not intend this world to be all there is. He had promised a future time when all the troubles of life—in particular, political enemies and the sinful behavior of the people—would be done away with. Then God's people would rule forever in a glorious kingdom in which God Himself would have an undefiled and open relationship with them.

It was all something far off, distant, at the end of time. Most of the Old Testament prophecies were vague about the timing; it would happen "on that day" (the day of judgment) or "at the end." It was certain; but it was not yet.

As a prophet, it would not have been at all unusual for Jesus to preach about God's kingdom. His preaching, however, had a dramatic twist: He said the kingdom was near! The long wait was over. The time was suddenly accelerating, and the climax was approaching. If the kingdom was so near, what would it be like? And how was it going to arrive?

The Parables of the Kingdom

 FINDING TRUTH

Read Mark 4:1-34.

1. Look back over verses 1-20. Jesus has been preaching the "good news of God" (1:14-15). What does the parable of the sower say about potential responses to the announcement of this news?

   Some will ignore
   Some will hear but fall easily.
   Some will hear but troubles overshad
   Some will hear and bear fruit.

2. Look back over verses 21-22.

   a. What does this parable lead you to expect?

      Jesus is the light of the world — we should also "shine".

   b. What does it say about Jesus' ministry?

      All will come to light and be explained.

3. The lesson of this parable is reinforced by the saying in verses 24-25. What is the promise and the warning of these verses?

   God will judge you by your standards
   Put effort into understanding the word and one will get more out of it. Practice what one hears.

4. Look back over verses 26-29.

   a. What does this parable lead you to expect?

      Sow the word and it will grow even if we don't understand how.

b. What does this say about the kingdom?

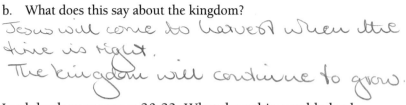

Jesus will come to harvest when the time is right. The kingdom will continue to grow.

5. Look back over verses 30-32. What does this parable lead you to expect?

The kingdom of God will grow grow a tiny beginning to cross all boundaries and nurture all peoples.

The World Tree

The "tree" image is used in other places in the Bible to stand for a kingdom. In Daniel 4:9-12, 19-22, a tree is the symbol of a kingdom that exercises world dominion (see also Ezek. 17:22-24). It is a tree that spreads its branches over all. In Mark 4, the largeness of the plant that grows from the mustard seed points to the worldwide spread of God's kingdom. As the Old Testament expected, the kingdom of God would involve all kinds of people and not just Israel—all the nations of the world would be included.

6. In summary, what would these parables lead you to expect?

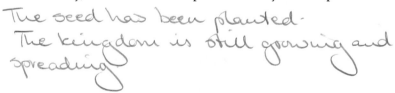

The seed has been planted. The kingdom is still growing and spreading.

The kingdom of God as taught by Jesus has some surprising characteristics. It is not going to come by political conquest or force; it has elements of secrecy and slow, hidden growth. At the same time, something about it is to be openly disclosed (vv. 22-23).

There is also a hint that some people will be inside the kingdom and some will be outside. There will be those like the bad soils, who either never listen at all (v. 15) or do not take it seriously (vv. 16-19); there will be those whose ears are closed, who will hear but never understand (v. 12). It is as if Jesus is saying that the kingdom is there for those who want it, but there will be those who will turn away.

The kingdom is certainly coming, says Jesus. It is inevitable, as surely as reaping follows sowing. We therefore need to get ready for it—urgently—if we are to be part of God's future.

 GOING FURTHER

1. What does the Gospel of Jesus say to a world filled with hopes and dreams for a better future?

A better future is coming

2. Why will some not listen? What is it about the kingdom that they do not like?

3. What might keep you from the kingdom? How can you prevent it from doing so?

The Sheep and Their Shepherds

MARK 4:35–7:8

One of the remarkable benefits of democracy is that it allows us regularly to remove our political leaders. We don't have to resort to civil war or royal beheadings. All it takes is a nice, orderly election, which is arranged for us by the political leaders themselves every few years.

It is curious that we feel the need for this constant changeover of leadership. Surely, on a purely practical level, it would make more sense for the leadership to be long-term, to have time to consolidate, to plan for the future and effect some real change. It seems, however, that we have an innate distrust of our leaders. Perhaps this is because they so regularly let us down. They do not keep their promises; they appear to act selfishly and not in the best interests of the country; indeed, we have political leaders these days who openly state that they lie as a matter of course.

This is not only a modern problem. Human leaders, whether political, religious, or social, have a sad history of corruption, failure, neglect, and self-interest. It was the same in the Israel of Jesus' time; but there it was even more serious, for Israel's leaders had a special mandate from God to look after His chosen people. Their failure, in contrast with Jesus, is the focus of this study.

Before we begin, a word of explanation about the next few studies: In this study and the next two, we will look at the large middle section of Mark that runs from 4:35 right through to the end of chapter 10. It's a little hard to divide these chapters up neatly into chunks for study, because the episodes are all so interconnected and gain much of their meaning in relation to one another. In order to get some feel for this, the passages we will read in this study and the next two will overlap with one another somewhat.

Jesus the Powerful Shepherd

 FINDING TRUTH

Read Mark 4:35-41.

1. What does this episode show us about Jesus' strength and authority?

   Power over all, even the elements.

2. Why do the disciples ask their question (v. 41)?

   Still didn't know who he was.

3. Of what were they afraid?

   Dying

Read Psalm 107:23-32.

4. How does this add meaning to Jesus' actions in the boat?

   Jesus will deliver us safely — we need to say thank you!

Read Mark 5:1-20.

5. In the description of the man, what is emphasized?

   His strength, the demons

6. Look back at Mark 3:23-27, where Jesus answers the accusation that He Himself is possessed by Satan. In light of this, what have we learned about Jesus from His encounter with the demoniac?

   He has the power over them.

7. Compare the words used to describe Jesus in Mark 5:19-20. Who did Mark think Jesus was?

   Mark says he is "Lord" and "god"

Jesus crosses back over the sea and is again confronted by a group of people who are suffering the physical effects of the fallen world. Again we see Jesus' strength. Read Mark 5:21-43.

8. Jairus is a synagogue ruler, one of the religious leaders of his people, yet he is powerless to save his daughter. What does he expect from Jesus? What does he get?

Healing
A miracle — raising her from the dead.

9. The woman with bleeding is also powerless and beyond the help of anyone else. What response does Jesus commend her for?

Her faith
He makes her a public witness.

Read Mark 6:1-6.

10. What is so strange about the response to Jesus in Nazareth?

Did not believe in him as they saw him growing up.

11. What are the reasons for the people's response?

Israel's Failed Shepherds

Immediately following these demonstrations of Jesus' strength, we have passages telling us about Israel's official leadership—first Herod (6:14-29) and then the Pharisees (7:1-16). And sandwiched in between these two passages about Israel's leaders, we again see the power and compassion of Jesus, the true and faithful Shepherd of Israel (6:30-56). Mark often uses this sort of device in his Gospel; we will see more of it in the coming chapters. He links together different incidents in order to make a point. He sets up contrasts and comparisons, sometimes between Jesus and the religious authorities, and sometimes between the disciples and other people who are responding to Jesus.

Lying very prominently in the background to this whole section is the prophecy of Ezekiel.

FINDING TRUTH

Read Ezekiel 34:1-6.

1. What should the shepherds of Israel have been doing?

   "Tending the flock."

2. What were they doing instead?

   Looking after themselves

3. What had happened to the sheep?

   They scattered.

4. Does anything in this passage sound like what Jesus has been doing?

   Jesus looked after and gathered in the sheep. He cared for them and wanted to heal.

Read Ezekiel 34:11-16, 20-24.

5. What did God promise to do for His flock?

   To look after the flock.

6. Whom would He send?

   His shepard.

Read Mark 6:14-29.

7. Is Herod an attractive or an unattractive character? What are his strengths and weaknesses?

   Immoral, Weak

   Intelligent, Keeps his word

8. What threat does Herod pose for Jesus' mission?

Read Mark 6:30-44.

9. What phrase in this passage reminds us of Ezekiel 34?

   Sheep without a shepard.

10. Look up Numbers 27:15-18. Given that "Joshua" is simply the Hebrew form of "Jesus," what is being said about Jesus in Mark 6?

    Jesus is the answer to Moses' plea for a shepard for his sheep. Joshua and Jesus both have the spirit.

11. How is Jesus being contrasted with Herod? What does Jesus do that Herod doesn't do?

    Jesus cares for the sheep — Herod not.

Read Mark 7:1-8.

12. What problem does Jesus expose in Israel's leaders?

    They stuck to the rules — but their hearts were not in it (worshipping God)

13. Why are the leaders hard-hearted?

    Teach man-made rules and do not want to change — not open to new teaching.

14. Overall, what is Jesus' assessment of Israel's leadership?

    Hypocrites
    Jesus was critical.

In Ezekiel 34, God promised to come to His people, to search for the lost, to gather the strays, and to feed them. He also promised to send another "David," another great shepherd-king who would care for his people.

Who then is Jesus? He is clearly portrayed in these chapters as God's alternative to the corrupt leadership of Israel. He is the one who has compassion on the scattered sheep. But is He the Lord who has come to gather His people? Or is He the "David," the Messiah, come to be their prince? Or is He perhaps both?

To this we turn in our next study.

 **GOING FURTHER**

1. What makes a leader worth following?

   Sincere, compassionate, achieve
   results, wisdom, has vision,
   Example,

2. What makes Jesus a leader worth following?

   He is the messiah and is
   the way to god
   He forgives and intercedes
   He is dependable.

3. What is the proper response to Him?

   Reverence, fellowship, devotion,
   gratitude, acknowledge and
   accept.
   Listen, obey, depend, wait

4. Why do people not give that response?

   other gods
   Pride - no need of him.
   Weakness - do not want to acknow-
               ledge him.

5

"Who Do You Say I Am?"

MARK 6:45–8:30

In our last study we saw the contrast between Jesus and Israel's leadership. With the arrival of Jesus, God is coming to replace the corrupt and failed leadership of Israel with His own good shepherd in the line of David.

All the while, we the readers know who Jesus really is. Mark has told us from the very first sentence of the book that Jesus is the Messiah, the King, who has come to bring God's long-awaited kingdom.

However, for the characters in the story—the disciples, the crowds, the people Jesus meets, His family, the religious authorities— it's not so simple. They are still trying to figure out exactly what is going on and just who this amazing man is. Some of them will get it right. Others won't.

This is another constant theme throughout these chapters: Will the characters come to understand who Jesus really is? In particular, will the disciples, with whom we identify most, put their trust in Jesus? Or will they be hard-hearted and go the way of the Pharisees? And what about us? How will we respond?

The Heart Problem

In chapter 6, Jesus crosses the sea for a second time with His disciples (as He did in 4:35-41 and will again in 8:13-21). Once again He astounds them by revealing Himself in a unique way.

FINDING TRUTH

1. Modern readers without a solid Old Testament background may miss some of the points that Mark makes as he describes this event. Read Mark 6:45-56 and then look up the following Old Testament references that add meaning to the incident. Remember that this is not a matter of proof-texting but of recognizing that Mark is deliberately using language (describing what Jesus actually did) that should bring Old Testament images to your mind. As the picture builds up, draw your own conclusions: Who is this man?

   ▲ He walks on the sea; compare Psalm 77:19.

   Moses & the Red Sea

   ▲ He is about to pass them by; compare Exodus 33:19, 22; 34:6.

   Gods goodness is passing by
   Disciples had to acknowledge Jesus for

   ▲ He provokes fear; compare Exodus 20:18-21. *him to*
   God is awesome and is *respond*
   aware of what scares us.

   ▲ He tells them not to fear; compare Isaiah 41:13; 43:1-3; 44:2.
   God will save us and be with
   us always.

   ▲ He says, "It is I," or, better translated, "I AM"; compare Exodus 3:14; Isaiah 41:4.

   ▲ He seems to calm the wind; compare Psalm 65:7; 107:25-30.

   We need to learn to rely on Jesus

2. Why do the disciples respond as they do (6:50-52)? What is their problem?

3. Reread the first sea-crossing incident in Mark 4:35-41. Have the disciples progressed at all in their understanding?

Now read Mark 7:1-30.

4. What is the real problem of the religious leaders?

Adhering to tradition rather than worshipping God.

5. How do Jesus' disciples compare with the religious leaders (remember 4:40; 6:52)?

Hearts were hardened

6. The woman from Syrian Phoenicia (7:24-30) is a Greek. As Jesus points out to her, she is a foreigner to Israel. She is one of the "dogs," one of the unclean with whom Jews were not to associate. Given all this, how does the woman's response to Jesus compare with those we have just seen? What is the state of her heart?

Israel was his main focus
Woman was happy with the "crumbs"
– humble and believing as compared
to the Leaders and other Jews.

Hearing and Sight Problems

 FINDING TRUTH

Read Mark 7:31–8:26.

1. In light of the previous mass feeding (6:30-44), what is your impression of the disciples during the feeding of the four thousand (8:1-12)?

Hadn't learnt from the first time.

2. When Jesus again crosses the sea with the disciples (8:13-21), what does He warn them about?

Yeast of the pharisees & Herod – Evil influence can contaminate like yeast causes bread dough to rise – opposite views are both bad

3. How do you think this danger might explain the difference between the two feedings (compare Mark 6:4-6)?

Disciples took for granted

4. What problems do the disciples have, according to Jesus?

Lack of faith – hard hearts and cannot see & hear.

5. What is unusual about the healing of the blind man (8:22-26)? How is this a picture of the disciples?

Blind man could see but not see clearly – disciples were the same. Two step healing process like faith growing

6. Look again at the stories (7:31–8:12 and 8:22-26) that surround this conversation in the boat (8:13-21). If the disciples are ever to understand, what must happen to them?

Why concerned about no bread – He has already provided – Have faith. No need to boast – perform away from the crowd. Will face opposition from Pharisees

The Solution

In the marvelous way that Mark weaves together the different strands of his account, a stunning picture emerges—not only of the compassionate majesty and power of Jesus but also of the quite incredible hostility of the religious authorities and the baffling stupidity of His closest associates.

The disciples just do not understand. God Himself has come among them, the promises of Scripture are being fulfilled, yet Jesus' own followers—like Israel's leaders—are too dull to see it. Both the deaf-mute and the blind man are pictures of the disciples. They have ears but do not hear. They have eyes but do not see. They need someone to heal them, to open the deaf ears and blind eyes.

Fortunately for the disciples, there is someone among them who can do just that; and this is just what happens in 8:27-30. Like the mute whom Jesus healed, Peter's tongue is loosened and he begins to speak plainly. He confesses what we (as readers) have known all along: "You are the Christ." At last, the disciples openly recognize who Jesus is.

This is the climax of the Gospel thus far. As we shall see, it is also the turning point, for from this point on the story takes an amazing twist.

 GOING FURTHER

1. We tend to think of the Pharisees as the "bad guys" in the story. But what would have been their standing in the community of their day? How do you think they would have been regarded? Respected leaders

Jesus will always provide more than enough.

2. The disciples were for a time just like the Pharisees and Herod. Have you seen people reacting to Jesus like this?

Argue against Jesus
Refuse to "see" who he is.

3. What is necessary before people can understand who Jesus is?

Acknowledging our need for Jesus.

4. How does this make you think about:

▲ your own knowledge of Jesus?

Truly blessed!!.

▲ how you can help other people who don't know Jesus?

Show this love as best we can. Be true to Him and your faith.

6

"What Must I Do?"

MARK 8:27–10:52

 STARTING OUT

1. Think about the most impressive Christian people you know. What makes them stand out?

   Obey.
   Happy / can cope   *Faithfulness*
   Not Materialistic
   Helpful

2. If you were to ask most people today, what would they say is the essence of "being a Christian"?

   Non-Christian – lead perfect life
   Christians – behave / follow Jesus

So far in Mark's story, we have witnessed the arrival of the King—that is, Jesus the Messiah. Even the slow-witted disciples have begun to realize this.

But what sort of kingdom is Jesus about to establish? How will He do it? And what does He want from His followers?

As we shall see in this study, these questions are all related. And as Jesus begins to answer them, the disciples are in for a surprise.

 **FINDING TRUTH**

Read Mark 8:27–9:1.

1. What does Peter now see (v. 29)?

   Jesus is Messiah

2. What does he not yet see (vv. 31-33)?

   That Jesus death was prophesised and had to be fulfilled.

3. What lies in front of Jesus?

   The crucifiction

4. What does He want from His followers?

5. Why would His followers possibly be ashamed of Jesus?

6. Why does Jesus make such an urgent demand?

   Time was short.

Read Mark 9:2-13.
7. On the mountain the three disciples are given a glimpse of Jesus' glory. What are they reminded about? (Compare 9:7 with 1:11.)

8. What will happen to Jesus?

The extraordinary events on the mountain only reinforce the message that the disciples have found so unacceptable—namely, that despite all His glory and power, and despite the fact that He is the Messiah, Jesus faces suffering, rejection, and death at the hands of Israel's leaders. It must happen, for Scripture says so.

Jesus points out to the disciples that the Elijah figure (John the

Baptist) has already come first, just as the Scriptures said he would, and that he has suffered at the hands of the very people who should have been expecting him. Therefore, the only thing left to happen before the kingdom of God arrives is that the Son of Man must also suffer. He will then rise from the dead, at which time the disciples can tell others what they had seen on the mountain (9:9).

True to their form thus far, the three disciples do not understand Jesus' teaching. They have not grasped why the Christ has to suffer. Peter would rather keep the glory while it is there (9:5)—he has not understood that glory must come by way of the Cross.

In the episodes that follow, this theme continues to be played out. Just what is the right response to Jesus? What does He want from His followers?

 FINDING TRUTH

Read Mark 9:14–10:52 and fill in the following table as you go.

Incident or Teaching	What attitude or response does Jesus commend?	What attitude or response does Jesus condemn?
Healing the boy (9:14-32)	Faith, prayer	Unbelief.
Who is the greatest? (9:33-37)	Servant	Wanting to be first
Against vs. for us (9:38-41)	Good things on his behalf	Stopping God's work. acceptance
Kingdom vs. hell (9:42-50)	Sinlessness	Sinning / bad habits
Pharisees and divorce (10:1-12)	Faithfulness in marriage	Adultery & divorce
The children (10:13-16)	Teaching of children	Lack of child-like faith.
The rich man (10:17-31)	Love God more than possessions	Material possession. the desire for.
Suffering and servanthood (10:32-45)	Servanthood.	Wanting to be first.
Blind Bartimaeus (10:46-52)	Faith	

 **GOING FURTHER**

Think back over this whole section (8:27–10:52).

1. What is Jesus' repeated message to the disciples about what must happen to Him before the kingdom comes?

2. What sort of Messiah is Jesus? How will He bring in His kingdom?

3. How is this related to entering the kingdom? What is the only way into the kingdom?

4. Who are the best examples of this response in this section?

5. Who are the worst examples?

Like the previous section of Mark's Gospel, this section also finishes with a blind man being healed—but there is an important difference between the two healings. The first blind man (8:22-26) is healed in two stages. At first he sees and yet does not quite see. This is a picture of the disciples. They finally realize that Jesus is the Messiah/Christ, yet they are still rather blurry about how He will bring in the kingdom and what they must do to enter it. They believe, and yet they need to overcome their unbelief (like the father of the boy with the evil spirit).

The second blind man (Bartimaeus, 10:46-52) is a model of true discipleship. He hears about Jesus, immediately asks for mercy, and having received it, follows Jesus along the road to Jerusalem where Jesus will be crucified.

The children are the same. They are not great or rich or powerful or prestigious. They simply come to Jesus seeking a blessing, and He receives them gladly. Their dependency and trust make them classic examples of what it means to enter the kingdom.

Woven throughout these examples of right and wrong responses to Jesus is the constant prediction by Jesus of His suffering and death. This culminates in 10:45, where Jesus explains that He has come as the "Servant" (as in Isaiah 53) who will give His life as a ransom for many. When He dies, it will be as a sacrifice for sins, to take away the debt that is owed, to pay the price of freedom for the many. This is the necessary cost of bringing in His kingdom, for if sinners are going to enter it, they must receive mercy; and if God is going to dispense mercy, then sin must be paid for.

In other words, this whole section links together two crucial ideas:

- ▲ that in defiance of people's expectations, the Messiah will bring in the kingdom by suffering, dying, and rising again as a ransom to pay for the sins of many;
- ▲ that in defiance of people's expectations, the way to enter the kingdom of Jesus is through humble dependence and faith; the way to be great in the kingdom is to be a lowly servant.

Not that this will be easy: Following Jesus means being willing to forgo anything that keeps us from the kingdom. We must be prepared to give up everything, lose everything, and depend only on Jesus. Our Christ was the one who died to become King. Being in the kingdom means going the way of the Cross. It will be hard, but it will be worth it.

GOING FURTHER

1. When we talk about "following Jesus" we normally mean something like obeying His teaching or following His example. What does following Jesus mean in this part of Mark? Where were people following Him *to?*

2. What does this mean for our own life? How would you summarize the essence of the Christian life having read this part of Mark's Gospel?

3. Throughout this section of Mark, what are the things that get in the way of people responding rightly to Jesus? Which of these is most relevant to you?

4. According to Jesus, true greatness in His kingdom lies in servanthood, just as He came not to be served but to serve. Think about how this might be worked out:

    ▲ in your own life and relationships with people

    ▲ in your church

7

He Overturned the Tables

MARK 11–12

 STARTING OUT

1. Every time someone has an opinion about Jesus, it means they are judging Him. For instance, some people say they will only believe Jesus is Lord if you can prove that it is reasonable and rational to do so. Think for a moment about how people judge Jesus. What standards or yardsticks do people use to judge Him?

   — human standards since that is all we know.

   — judge Jesus by "believers" actions

Chapters 11 and 12 of Mark's Gospel cover three days of action in Jerusalem. As Jesus interacts with people, we begin to see that judging Jesus can be a dangerous business. He has a habit of turning the tables and putting His accusers in the dock.

Day One: The Coming King

 FINDING TRUTH

Read Mark 11:1-11.

1. What does Jesus do on Day One?

   Rides into Jerusalem on a donkey.

2. What are people expecting when He arrives in Jerusalem? (Compare Zechariah 9:9.)

   Prophecy was fulfilled Expecting Him to declare Himself king.

Day Two: The Ruined Kingdom?

 FINDING TRUTH

Read Mark 11:12-19.

1. What does Jesus do on Day Two?

   Fig tree — Israel's unfruitfulness. Clears the temple — forcing the issue with the leaders.

2. What impression of Israel do these events convey?

   Israel moving away from God

3. Look up the two Old Testament passages quoted in verse 17 to see what light they shed on the events:

   a. Isaiah 56:4-8. What should the temple have been for?

   b. Jeremiah 7:1-11. Whom was Jeremiah prophesying against, and what were they doing wrong?

4. Whom is Jesus criticizing?

   The religious leaders.

At first glance, the cursing of the fig tree (11:12-14, 20-21) seems quite bizarre. Why would Jesus do such a thing?

Like so many of the incidents recorded in Mark's Gospel, the cursing of the fig tree takes its meaning partly from its Old Testament background and partly from its place in the story Mark is telling. In Micah 7, a fruitless grapevine is likened to Israel, in which there is not one godly person. Sure enough, in Mark 11, immediately after Jesus curses the barren fig tree, He enters Jerusalem only to find it equally unprepared for His arrival. Jerusalem too is barren. Instead of the temple being a house of prayer, it is a den of robbers. Corruption is rampant. Instead of the temple being a beacon for the nations and for all the outcast to come and meet the Lord, it has become a place of empty ritual and commercial greed. The Lord arrives at His temple and finds His people blind to His identity and presence. They are more interested in making a buck!

The Old Testament prophets laid the blame for Israel's decline on Israel's leaders, and it appears that Jesus agrees. The high priests and their entourage are especially singled out for His wrath. Israel's leadership has let Israel down. As with the fig tree, it was "not the season for fruit," because Israel's leadership has caused Israel's ruin.

Day Three: Who Is the Judge?

 FINDING TRUTH

Read Mark 11:27–12:44.

1. Jot down a quick summary of what happens on Day Three.

- Demonstrating how powerful he
was

2. Fill in this table:

	How do they attack Jesus?	On what basis does Jesus reply?	What is the outcome?
Teachers of the law and elders	By whose authority does He clear the temple	Asks a question	Stalemate — Amazement
Pharisees and Herodians	Should they pay tax?	Give to Ceasar what is his and to god what is God's	''
Sadducees			God is god the living & not the dead.

3. Overall, who is the victor thus far? Do you expect that this
   will be the end of the conflict?

   Jesus — no.

4. What is different about the teacher's question in 12:28?

   Did not try to trap Jesus — he wanted to learn.

The tension between Jesus and the religious leaders, simmering
throughout Mark's Gospel, is now exploding into full-scale conflict.
For His part, Jesus warns people that the religious leaders are dangerous hypocrites. They are even "devouring" the houses of wid-
ows—the very people that Israel's leaders were supposed to especially
protect. The little incident at the temple treasury (12:41-44) is a
case in point. Here is a widow whose house literally is being
devoured; while the rich are relatively unaffected by their large dona-
tions, she has to put everything she has into paying the religious
authorities' temple tax. Israel's leadership is ruining Israel!

Jesus defeats Israel's leaders and obviously knows more about
the Christ than they do. He appears to be firmly in charge throughout the whole day's activities. And yet we have still ringing in our ears
Jesus' predictions (in chapters 8–10) that these same leaders will
eventually persecute and kill Him. The irony is that in thus judging
Jesus, they will be judged themselves:

> "What then will the owner of the vineyard do? He will come and
> kill those tenants and give the vineyard to others. Haven't you read
> this scripture: 'The stone the builders rejected has become the cap-
> stone; the Lord has done this, and it is marvelous in our eyes'?"
> (Mark 12:9-11).

GOING FURTHER

1. How do the events of chapters 11–12 illustrate Mark 4:24-25?

2. Why do people reject Jesus today?

   people do not want to commit

3. The really important question these chapters pose is: What is our judgment of Jesus? How would you answer the question in Mark 11:28?

   He does it by God's authority.

8

"When Will These Things Happen?"

MARK 13

"Show Me a Sign"

Perhaps it stems from our longing for certainty about the future, or it might be simply a result of our unfailing human curiosity, but passages such as Mark 13 have always held a particular fascination for Christians—along with parts of Daniel, Zechariah, Ezekiel, 2 Thessalonians, and Revelation. Whenever the Bible addresses the future of human history, and speaks somewhat cryptically of when and how it will unfold, we cannot help ourselves. We instinctively want to unlock the mystery, decipher the symbols, and work out exactly what will happen and when. Indeed, Christian history is littered with the strange doctrines, millennial speculations, schisms, and controversies that have arisen from the intensity of this desire to know the future.

The disciples of Jesus certainly have the future in mind when they leave Jerusalem at the beginning Mark 13. Things don't look so good between Jesus and the religious authorities. Trouble is brewing. The predictions of Jesus about His suffering and death, so strange and unthinkable in chapter 8, now seem more likely if not inevitable.

One of the disciples tries to comfort Jesus by referring to the majesty of the temple. However, as Jesus responds and the conversation continues, it becomes apparent that once again the disciples don't really know what's going on.

FINDING TRUTH

Read Mark 13:1-4.

1. Why would the disciple have considered his remark (v. 1) to be an encouraging thing to say to Jesus? (Psalm 48:12-14 will help you answer this.)

   Comforting Jesus that the temple will prevail.

2. How do you think Jesus' reply (v. 2) would have been received by the disciples? How is this reflected in their double-barreled question of verse 4?

   Disbelief—want to know more.

3. Compare Mark 8:11-13. Is this the sort of question the disciples should have been asking? Is there anything wrong with their attitude?

Read Mark 13:5-13.

4. What danger does Jesus warn the disciples about?

   False Messiah.

5. What specific difficulties will they face?

   Battles, earthquakes, famines.

6. Why would these difficulties make Jesus' warning all the more important?

7. What will keep the disciples going?

   Stand firm

Read Mark 13:14-23.

8. What are the disciples told to do when they see the awful horror of verse 14? Why the urgency?

9. In this time of great distress, there will be people who offer a dangerous threat to the disciples. Why are they such a threat? (vv. 21-22; compare 8:27-30)

False prophets

10. In view of the troubled times that lay ahead for them, why is the disciples' original question (v. 4) a dangerous one? (Compare vv. 21-23.)

If the disciples thought that the destruction of the temple was an alarming prospect, Jesus tells them, "You ain't seen nothin' yet!" The catastrophe that is coming will involve the greatest time of distress this world has ever seen or will ever see (v. 19). It will be so severe that the Lord will have to limit it for the sake of the elect (v. 20). Daniel had been told about this great distress before the end-time resurrection (Dan. 12:1-4). He had been told that this would happen a long way in the future (Dan. 12:9), but now the disciples are told that they would experience these things in their own lifetime!

The book of Daniel is much in the background of this passage. The "abomination that causes desolation" of Mark 13:14 is an allusion to Daniel 9:27, 11:31, and 12:11. When Jesus says, "Let the reader understand," He probably means, "understand that what Daniel spoke of, I am now warning you about." The emphasis is upon the "abomination" or "horror" or "sacrilege." Jesus is warning the disciples that something absolutely horrendous is coming . . . and soon.

Jesus returns to His warning (v. 23), which shows that this has been His concern for the entire passage so far. The disciples asked a "sign-seeking question" (v. 4) and this is why Jesus warns them so sternly. In the difficult times to come, there would be people who would deny their previous recognition of Jesus as the Christ, and who might even offer signs to back up their claims (compare Deut. 13:1-5). If the disciples were sign-seekers, this would be a powerful temptation for them to desert Jesus as their Christ, especially given that this temptation would come at a time of severe personal distress.

Jesus resets the disciples' sights. Rather than looking out for signs (v. 4) or for "proof" of what is going to happen, they are to have certain general expectations. They are to be on the alert for the catastrophic things that are about to take place.

 FINDING TRUTH

1. List the things Jesus says the disciples will see, and any references to timing of these things:

    ▲ verses 14-23:

    Abomination of desolation.

    ▲ verses 24-25:

    Sun will no longer shine

    ▲ verse 26:

    Son of Man will come

    ▲ verse 27:

    ▲ verses 28-29:

    ▲ verse 30:

    ▲ verse 32:

2. Read Mark 13:32-37. Since the exact timing of these things is unknown, what should the disciples do?

Watch and be prepared

When Will "These Things" Happen?

Although the disciples were wrong to ask for "signs" or proofs of what was to happen in the future, it wasn't wrong for them to ask "when." Jesus seems happy to answer that question, and He does so by saying, "No one knows exactly when, but it's not far away—and certainly within your lifetime."

This has led Christians to puzzle over exactly what Jesus meant. Was He talking about the end of the world? Those who think that He was take verse 26 ("At that time men will see the Son of Man coming in clouds with great power and glory") to refer to the second coming of Christ. Verses 5-23 then become a description of the great distress which is to precede this event, including the coming of the Antichrist who is symbolically referred to as "the abomination of desolation" (v. 14). The difficulty with this view, of course, is that Jesus solemnly declares in verse 30 that these events will happen within the lifetime of that generation . . . and they plainly didn't.

The other main approach to the passage says that verse 26 should be read in the same way as Daniel 7:13-14—that is, that the Son of Man comes to God, not to earth. This would then apply to the resurrection, ascension, and exaltation of Jesus. However, this view then goes on to say that Jesus' exaltation is demonstrated through the destruction of Jerusalem in A.D. 70. Verses 5-23 are taken to describe the lead-up to the destruction of Jerusalem, and it is only at verse 32 that Jesus begins to speak about His second coming. This approach has two problems: first, it gives enormous and somewhat dubious theological weight to the destruction of Jerusalem, a historical event beyond the time of Jesus; and second, it has Jesus changing the subject (from the destruction of the temple to His second coming) without any real indication in the text that He is doing so.

These two approaches to the difficulties of Mark 13 have this in common: They look for the solution *outside* of Mark's Gospel (either in the return of Christ or in the destruction of Jerusalem). But given how cleverly and purposefully Mark has told his story up till now, why would he break the spell at this crucial point? Why would he start addressing other events quite beyond the lifetime of Jesus? Is it possible that the predictions and warnings of Mark 13 actually refer to what is about to happen next in the story?

A careful reading of the text (and the rest of the story that follows) shows that this is very possible. It is right to take verse 26 as referring to the resurrection and exaltation of Jesus (which Jesus has already predicted in earlier chapters), but there is no need to interpret verses 5-23 as being about the fall of Jerusalem. According to the passage, this time of horrendous distress and appalling sacrilege will happen before the "coming of the Son of Man." What terrible event—the worst event in human history—was to happen before the exaltation of Jesus? Put like this, the answer seems obvious: that Israel's leaders should reject, mock, and persecute their Messiah and hand Him over to the Gentiles to be humiliated, flogged, and crucified. What could be more desolating and abominable than the death of God's own Son at the hands of God's own people?*

If this way of reading Mark 13 is right, then verses 32-37 also make good sense. In warning the disciples to be on their guard, Jesus refers to the four watches of the night: evening, midnight, cockcrow, and dawn. These four time references provide the structure for the chapters that follow. Jesus meets with the disciples in the upper room at "evening" (14:17); He agonizes in Gethsemane and is betrayed in the middle of the night (14:32-42); He is deserted by His closest friends at "cock-crow" (14:72); and the women go to His empty tomb at "dawn" (16:2).

*There is not room here to explore this view in any detail. To pursue it further, see P. G. Bolt, "Mark 13: An Apocalyptic Precursor to the Passion Narrative," *Reformed Theological Review*, 54.1, 1995, 10-32. This view is based to a large extent on the idea that the language of Mark 13 is "apocalyptic" in style, like parts of Daniel. This was a well-known way of writing in the ancient world. It was used to move the reader emotionally by using strong and vivid imagery—imagery that may not be meant to be taken as historical.

Lessons for the Future

Regardless of how we interpret the details, Mark 13 has some important lessons for us about how we regard the future and how we deal with the suffering and difficulty that inevitably awaits us.

First, we must be wary of the attitude that looks for a sign. To demand a sign is itself a sign—of unbelief. Like the disciples (and unlike the Pharisees) we must trust in Jesus and believe what He tells about the future. And we must do so without demanding confirmation through signs.

Second, we must expect our future to include suffering. Whenever Christians try to stand firm for the Gospel there will be hardship. There will always be false Christs trying to lead us astray. We need to watch out, as the disciples did, and remember that Jesus' promises are still true.

 GOING FURTHER

1. What examples do you see today of people looking for signs to confirm God's promises? What is tempting about such signs?

2. What examples have you come across of detailed speculation about the future and efforts to interpret Bible prophecies in terms of current world events? What do you think Jesus would say to those who engage in such speculation?

3. What did the disciples have to do to keep living for Jesus despite the difficulties they faced?

4. If you live as a Christian, what difficulties will you face while waiting for the future that Jesus promises?

5. What makes it worth enduring such difficulties?

6. What does Jesus say to our modern world about the future?

9

"The Hour Has Come!"

MARK 14:1–15:39

As Jesus and His disciples have moved toward Jerusalem, the tension has mounted. Many people hate Him and want Him killed. Moreover, Jesus Himself has said that in Jerusalem He will be killed. When He arrives in Jerusalem, the tension increases further, for Jesus makes His opponents look foolish, which only makes them hate Him all the more.

Now the sword that has been hanging over Jesus' head falls.

What will Jesus' followers do? Will they stand firm, as they insisted so many times they would? Will they heed the warning of chapter 13 and remain alert? Will the crowds who loved Him take His side? Or will they disown Jesus for fear of the authorities? Will God intervene and somehow save His Messiah, or will the unthinkable happen?

As we read these two long and harrowing chapters, these questions are raised and answered. It is a story full of tension and drama, but Mark is not interested in merely telling a good story. As we watch what the people in the Gospel do, we are forced to ask: What will *we* do?

Others Prepare for Jesus' Death

FINDING TRUTH

Read Mark 14:1-11.

1. What do the priests, the woman, and Judas have in common?

Preparing Him for death.

2. What does Judas give the authorities that they have been looking for?

A chance to get Jesus.

3. What do you think of Judas' action? Does the passage hint at his motives?

Dishonesty, jealousy, ambition, tried to get Jesus to "become King", devil-driven

Jesus Prepares for His Death

 FINDING TRUTH

Read Mark 14:12-25.

1. What different reactions are there to Jesus' announcement that He will be betrayed?

Each thought it may be them. Surprise.

2. Why is the betrayal particularly tragic?

*One of their own
The impact on Judas.*

The Passover

In Exodus 11–13, the Israelites were at the point of escaping from their slavery in Egypt. God had already sent terrible plagues on Egypt to persuade Pharaoh to let them go free, but Pharaoh had consistently refused. Finally, God was going to send the last and most terrible judgment: Every firstborn son in every household would be killed. The Israelites, however, were told to sacrifice a lamb and paint its blood on their doorposts so that the destroying angel would know who were God's people and would "pass over" their houses. The people of Israel would be saved from God's judgment.

Lamb – blood   Salt, water – tears
Bread – hurried   Bitter herbs – bitterness
– bricks with straw

4 cups wine – 4 promises,

Ever since that event, the Israelites were to remember their salvation from Egypt each year by celebrating the Passover feast.

3.   How does Jesus reinterpret this Passover meal?

His body and blood.

4.   If this is the new meaning of the Passover, what do you expect to happen to Jesus if He is the new Passover Lamb?

He will be sacrificed

5.   What is the significance of Jesus' promise in 14:25?

Confirms his death
He will be in the Kingdom.

"The Hour Has Come!"

 FINDING TRUTH

Read Mark 14:27-31.

1.   What does Jesus predict will happen:

▲   to Himself?

▲   to His followers?

2. What do you think of Peter's protestations? Do you feel positive or negative toward him?

Read Mark 14:32-42.
3. What is the struggle facing the disciples? How do you react to them?

4. What is the struggle facing Jesus? How do you react to Him?

5. What does the arrival of Judas indicate?

Read Mark 14:43-52.
6. How do you end up feeling toward:
   ▲ the disciples?

   ▲ Judas?

   ▲ Jesus?

Read Mark 14:53-72.

7.   Why is it a surprise to find Peter still following Jesus?

8.   At His trial, what is Jesus condemned for?

9.   What does Jesus promise?

10. What does Peter's denial (vv. 66-72) indicate:
     ▲   about him?

     ▲   about Jesus?

     ▲   about Jesus' other promises?

The Hour of Judgment

FINDING TRUTH

Read Mark 15:1-39.

1.   Why was Jesus killed? What reasons can you find?

Envy - Priests.
He said He was the king of the Jews

2. How do these reasons fit together?

3. How do you feel toward these characters and why?
   ▲ Pilate
   He was weak — pressured

   ▲ the crowd
   Mob mentality.

   ▲ the religious leaders
   threatened their power base.

   ▲ the disciples (they aren't even present!)
   unknowing, outnumbered.

   ▲ the Gentile centurion (15:39)
   thinking man — came to believe.

4. Do you feel close to or distant from Jesus?
   Close to His aloneness
   not confident enough to take steps

5. What is the effect of all this? What does the story make you want to do?
   appreciate the sacrifice.
   react better than His accusers.
   live as Jesus would have us do.

Our familiarity with the story of Jesus' death can blind us to what a shocking narrative it is. It is a heart-wrenching story, and we cannot help wondering why they would do this to Jesus. The way the story is told makes us feel repulsed at everyone who has betrayed or mistreated or abused Jesus. And yet, curiously, as the story proceeds we can also feel distant from Jesus Himself, as if we too have deserted Him on the Cross.

This is the climax of the Gospel. These are the events the whole story has been leading toward, and which Jesus has predicted with increasing urgency since chapter 8. In chapters 14–15, two of the main themes of Mark's Gospel come together. First, Jesus is clearly crucified as the Messiah or "King of Israel." This is the charge the Sanhedrin finds Him guilty of; this is the taunt the soldiers hurl at Him; and this is the sign mockingly nailed above His head. Israel's King has come to His people, and yet they have rejected Him and handed Him over to the Gentiles to be killed.

Second, Jesus dies as the Suffering Servant who gives His life to save His people. Note the bitter irony of the taunts: "He saved others . . . but he can't save himself!" (v. 31). Jesus' enemies are unwittingly expressing the very heart of what is taking place. Jesus is in fact dying to save others, as a "ransom for many." He is drinking the cup of God's judgment, being forsaken by His Father, so that He could open up access to God for all His people (symbolized in the tearing of the temple curtain).

In yet another ironic touch, the crucifixion concludes with the confession of the pagan centurion. He alone of all those present recognizes what we the readers have known from the very beginning: that Jesus is the Son of God! And yet he comes to this realization as he witnesses how Jesus died.

The challenge we are left with is, will his response be our response?

GOING FURTHER

1. What makes Jesus attractive in these chapters?

    His humility and willingness to die.
    Human traits - fear, questioning,

2. Why did Jesus have to die?

    To prove God's dominance over death.
    To remove the barrier between us and God.

3. What is the right response to Jesus' death? How do we receive the benefits of Jesus' death?

    Gratitude

4. Have you claimed for yourself the benefits of Jesus' death?

10

"He Is Not Here!"

MARK 15:40–16:8

Somewhere beyond the barricade,
Is there a world you long to see?

These lines from the musical *Les Miserables* express the human long-ing for a new and better world. We all want justice and peace, and a better place where suffering is no more.

According to Mark's Gospel, however, a new world has already begun—God's new world. And for excitement and grandeur, nothing compares with it.

The End of Jesus?

 FINDING TRUTH

Read Mark 15:40-41.

1. Do you identify with the women? Explain your response.

2. What do they do?

Followed Jesus and cared for Him

Read Mark 15:42-46.
3. Do you identify with Joseph? Explain your response.

*Wanted to do something practical
He showed compassion.*

4. What have we, the readers, been waiting for that Joseph is also waiting for? (Compare 1:15; 4:26-32; 9:1; 13:29; 14:25.)

The Kingdom of God.

5. What happens to these expectations now that Jesus is buried?

Disappointment and doubt as it would seem that the predications would not come to pass

Read Mark 16:1-8.
6. What is the significance of what the women find? Look up:
    ▲ Mark 9:31

    Jesus had risen as promised

    ▲ Mark 10:33-34

    Jesus will rise.

▲ Mark 13:24-26 (compare Dan. 7:13-14)

He rose and will rise to heaven.

▲ Mark 14:62

Jesus will sit at the right side of God.

7. If these expectations have now been fulfilled, what should happen next? Look back over:

▲ Mark 1:16-18

The disciples were to carry on after Him.

▲ Mark 9:9

After He had risen, they could teach.

▲ Mark 13:26-27

Son of Man will come in clouds to gather the believers

▲ Mark 14:9

Woman with perfume will be remembered.

▲ Mark 14:28

He told the disciples he would go to Galilee after his death

8. What does happen next? (16:8)

The women were afraid

9. Was the women's response right or wrong? Do you feel like condemning or rebuking them? Explain your response.

No as they were afraid

10. What is the effect of this last verse in Mark?*

*The earliest manuscripts do not include Mark 16:9-20.

Just the Beginning

"He has risen! He is not here," the man dressed in white says. And then we know that the expectations and predictions have all come true. The Son of Man has risen after His fiery ordeal (remember 10:33-34). He has come to the Ancient of Days (remember 13:24-26) and is now seated at the right hand of God (remember 14:62). Jesus' enemies have been shown to be wrong!

The man in white instructs the women to tell Jesus' disciples to meet Him in Galilee, exactly where Jesus had predicted (14:28). Now that the resurrection has happened, it is a time for telling people what was previously kept secret (9:9), a time for taking the Gospel to the world (13:10; 14:9), a time for the elect to be gathered (13:27), a time for the disciples to start their fishing for people (1:16-20), a time for the Gospel of Jesus Christ the Son of God to be proclaimed. Mark's story has led up to this moment. But it is not the end; it is just the beginning.

What do we think of the women? With this great command to speak the Good News of Jesus, the point to which the whole story has been leading, they are silent and afraid! Their silence is wrong, of course, but we can sympathize. We too know the experience of fear, especially when we know we should speak up for Christ and His Gospel. Yet silence is wrong, because after the resurrection is a time for Gospel proclaiming. The reaction of the women challenges us to think about our own silence. Even if we're afraid, it is still time to speak, because there is an empty tomb, Christ has risen, the kingdom of God has arrived!

In God's plan for this world there is only one event left to come. Jesus will return to share the kingdom of God with His people. The time between His resurrection and His return is a time for the Gospel to be proclaimed, so that people from all nations can be invited to enter the kingdom of God now, before it is too late. This Gospel is still being proclaimed, some thirty lifetimes later.

Mark has told us where it all began: It began with Jesus Christ, the Son of God. He came with a mission. His mission continues. Will you join Him in His mission?

 GOING FURTHER

1. What are the consequences of following Jesus in this modern world?

   Persecution
   Peace and mind
   Go against the norm.

2. What are the costs?

   Ridicule, ostracised.
   We are seen as different.

3. What are the benefits?

   Peace
   Different sense of values

4. If all that Mark says is true, how does it change:
   ▲ our dreams for the future of the world?

   that there will be world peace.

   ▲ our hopes and ambitions for our own future?

   ▲ our whole view of the world and what life is all about?

   material things are not important.

Tips for Leaders

Studying a book such as Mark presents particular problems for the small group leader. Not only are the passages longer than we might be used to studying (compared with, say, one of Paul's letters), but the way the Gospels communicate their message is a little different as well. They are narratives, using the techniques of storytelling to make their point. They need to be read and studied with this in mind.

This will mean paying very careful attention to how the different episodes lead into each other, how themes or incidents from early in the story pop up again later on, how the different characters in the story relate to each other and are contrasted, how the physical action of the characters gives structure to the story (such as the three sea crossings in Mark), whether markers of time and place are important, and so on.

We have tried to model this approach in the studies, but it may still go against the grain for some of those in your group. As the leader, you will need to guard against the instinct to take the familiar stories out of context, or to treat them as separate entities, each with their own "moral." Another common tendency is to read theology from elsewhere in the Bible (especially in the epistles) back into the Gospel stories. It is not as if Mark will contain a different theology, but we do need to let the book speak for itself, with its own particular concerns and emphases.

In terms of a commentary that might help in your preparation, we would recommend *The Gospel of Mark,* by William L. Lane, which is part of the New International Commentary on the New Testament (Grand Rapids, Mich.: Eerdmans, 1994).

FAITHWALK
BIBLE STUDIES

Ask your local bookstore about these other
FaithWalk Bible Studies

Old Testament
God's Unfolding Promise

Beginnings
Eden and Beyond: Genesis 1–11

Deuteronomy
The Lord Your God

Isaiah
The Road to God

Daniel
Our Faithful God

The Beatitudes
A Guide to Good Living: Matthew 5:1-12

Galatians
The Gospel of Grace

Ephesians
Our Blessings in Christ

Colossians
Continuing in Christ

1 Timothy
The Household of God

James
Life in the Real World

Notes

About Matthias Media

This Bible study guide, part of the *FaithWalk Bible Studies,* was originally developed and published in Australia by Matthias Media. Matthias Media is an evangelical publisher focusing on producing resources for Christian ministry. For further information about Matthias Media products, visit their website at: www.matthiasmedia.com.au; or contact them by E-mail at: matmedia@ozemail.com.au; or by fax at: 61-2-9662-4289.